CRAFT

IDEAS FOR 4s AND 5s

Craft Ideas for 4s & 5s II
DAVID C. COOK PUBLISHING CO.
Elgin, Illinois/Weston, Ontario
CRAFT IDEAS FOR 4s & 5s II
© 1990 David C. Cook Publishing Co.

Published by David C. Cook Publishing Co.
850 North Grove Avenue, Elgin, IL 60120
Cable address: DCCOOK
ISBN: 1-55513-213-8

Project Editor
Scottie May

Editors
Robin Currie
Dave and Neta Jackson
Ramona Warren

Designer
Dawn Lauck

Illustrator
Barbara Todd

Contributing Writers
Nancy Brown
Sherry Butler
Anna Marie Dahlquist
Carl Heine
Bob Klausmeier
Debbie Trafton O'Neil
Brenda and Donald Ratcliff
Anna Trimiew
Ramona Warren
Phyllis Wezeman
Colleen Wiessner

Little hands love to be busy! Fat crayons, glue sticks, and construction paper in lots of colors invite children to become creative. With a little planning these objects can do more than just keep preschoolers busy!

Making crafts can help young children feel good about things they create and help them learn to use their hands in new ways. Crafts can also remind preschoolers of what they've learned about God and what He has done. That's what the crafts in this book are designed to do!

Each of these 53 crafts reinforces a theme about God that is appropriate for 4s and 5s. Use these ideas whenever you want to teach young children about God—in children's church, Sunday school, mid-week club, day care—even at home. Some crafts include patterns which you may photocopy. All require only readily available, inexpensive supplies.

Let *Craft Ideas for 4s and 5s* help you remind preschoolers of special things about God. You'll enjoy leading 4s and 5s to praise God through the works of their hands!

"GOD MADE THEM" BUTTONS

Copy one circle for each child. Also, have available a 2 1/2" circle of cardboard or stiff paper and a small safety pin for each child. Let the children color the sun, moon, stars, and words. You might let the children spread glue on the stars and add glitter. Let the children cut out the circles. Then help them glue the picture circles to the cardboard or stiff paper circles. Tape the small safety pins to the backs of the cardboard or stiff paper. Read the words on the button to the children, and then have them say it with you as you pin the buttons on them. *May use stickers and sparkles.*

THINGS YOU'LL NEED:

- ❏ Copies of the "God Made Them" circles
- ❏ 2 1/2" circles of cardboard or stiff paper
- ❏ Small safety pins
- ❏ Glue
- ❏ Crayons or markers
- ❏ Glitter
- ❏ Tape

2 GOD'S WORLD PLAQUES

In advance, photocopy and cut out Bible verse half-circles for each child. Make several cardboard shapes for the water, land, and sky.

Let the children trace around the sky shapes on light blue construction paper, the land shapes on green or brown construction paper, and the water shapes on dark blue construction paper.

Have them cut out one each of the three pieces.

Give each child a large and small paper plate. Help children glue the light blue paper circles to the center of the small paper plates, then the "land" to the blue circles, and finally the "water" on top of that.

Give each child a copy of the Bible verse and show children how to glue the verse above and below the picture of water, sky, and land.

Help the children fold the large paper plate in half and tape the small paper plate to the large plate so that half of the small paper plate is above the fold. Glue the bottom half to the large one for additional strength.

Open the bottom of the large paper plate slightly to create a stand-up plaque.

THINGS YOU'LL NEED:

- ❑ Regular-sized paper plates (about 9" in diameter) and pie-sized paper plates (about 6" in diameter) Select the "flatter" variety.
- ❑ Light blue, dark blue, and green or brown construction paper
- ❑ Glue
- ❑ Scissors
- ❑ Cardboard shapes for sky, land, and water

use maybe a bird, animal of fish sticker in appropriate area.

Shapes are shown at a 50% reduction

SKY

LAND

WATER

In the beginning God...

created the heavens and the earth.

SOME THINGS GOD MADE

3

Help the children praise God for trees and plants by making a "Some Things God Made" booklet. In advance, make cardboard shapes of the flower, fruit, and vegetable patterns provided here.

Give the children each two sheets of white ~~colored~~ construction paper. Show them how to fold the sheets in half and nest one inside the other to make a booklet. Punch two holes several inches apart along the folded edge of their booklets. Help the children tie the booklet together by threading a length of yarn through the holes.

In large bold letters, print in the upper half of the cover of each child's book the words, "Some Things God Made." Let each child glue a dried leaf (if available) on the cover of the book below the title.

Then, using the colored construction paper, show the children how to trace the flowers, fruits, and vegetables with the cardboard shapes. Encourage red for cherries, yellow for corn, etc. Have them cut out the patterns and glue them on pages in the book. *or have them color them*

The children might like to add other drawings of plants and trees to their booklet pages. Be sure their names are on the back of the booklets.

THINGS YOU'LL NEED:

- ❑ Two pieces of 8 1/2" x 11" white construction paper for each child
- ❑ Various colors of construction paper
- ❑ Colored yarn
- ❑ Hole punch
- ❑ Several cardboard shapes of the flower, fruit, and vegetable patterns
- ❑ Pencils for tracing around shapes
- ❑ Crayons of various colors
- ❑ Dried, colorful fall leaves (optional)

4 WINKIE BEAR PICTURE FRAME

In advance, photocopy on stiff paper the pattern of Winkie Bear, and then cut out the square in the center of the picture frame that Winkie is holding. Use the pattern shape to cut out a back for each frame

Let the children color Winkie Bear and cut him out. Help each child staple the front and back together along the sides and across the bottom. Leave the top open so that a picture can be inserted. Also, do not staple at the neck area as this would constrict the top opening and prevent the insertion of the photograph.

While the children are working on Winkie Bear and the frame, take instant pictures of each child that can be slipped into their frames before they go home. Put a final staple through the side of the frame and the edge of the picture to prevent it from slipping out.

If an instant camera isn't available, the children can take home their picture frames and insert a photo from home.

If you have one to use great - give me the reciept for the film - you will be reimbursed!

THINGS I CAN DO

In advance, cut off the tops of white lunch bags, one for each child, as shown in the sketch. Use the part cut off for a handle. Staple the handle to the bag.

Instruct the children to draw a happy face on a piece of construction paper and then cut it out. Have them use a black crayon or marker for a nose and eyebrows. They should cut a smiling mouth from a different color of construction paper. Help them glue on the mouth and then glue the happy faces onto the paper bags. They might also add yarn for hair.

On the other side of the bag help them print the words, "Things I Can Do."

Have available slips of paper. Ask each child to tell you one thing he or she knows how to do. Print what children say on slips of paper and put them in the bags. Tell the children that at home they can have their parents print other things they can do on slips of paper and put them in the bag.

When a week has passed, they will be surprised at how many things they can do.

THINGS YOU'LL NEED:

- ❑ White lunch bags for each child
- ❑ Stapler
- ❑ Various colors of construction paper
- ❑ Scissors
- ❑ Pencils
- ❑ Glue
- ❑ Black crayon or marker
- ❑ Brightly colored yarn

GOD MADE EACH FAMILY MEMBER DIFFERENT

THINGS YOU'LL NEED:

- ❏ Photocopies of the family house for each child plus a few extras
- ❏ Sheets of very light blue construction paper
- ❏ Scissors
- ❏ Glue
- ❏ Pencils
- ❏ Crayons

Photocopy the house pattern for each child. Make extra copies so that children with larger families can have extra windows.

Instruct the children to cut off the windows along the solid line at the top of their sheet and cut them apart. Be sure to warn the children *not* to cut along the dotted line. Provide extra windows for those who need them. Show the children how to fold the windows back along the dotted line on the side of each window

The children should then cut out their houses and glue them onto construction paper. Then have them glue as many windows onto their houses as there are members in their families.

When the windows are opened, they can draw a picture of each family member in a window.

The whole picture can then be colored and enhanced with grass, flowers, trees, etc. Tip: It will make for a neater appearing house if it is colored *before* it is cut out or windows are glued on. Special decorating should be done at the end, however.

9 GET-ALONG-TOGETHER CLOWN

THINGS YOU'LL NEED:

- ❑ Lunch-size paper bags
- ❑ Old newspapers
- ❑ Stapler
- ❑ Large black marker
- ❑ Cardboard shapes for the clown's head, eyes, nose, mouth, and hat
- ❑ Pencils
- ❑ Scissors
- ❑ Various colors of construction paper
- ❑ Cotton balls
- ❑ Glue

In advance, prepare cardboard shapes for the clown's head, eyes, nose, and mouth that the children can trace around. Then, using a large black marker, print the words, "Get Along Together" on the paper bags for the children.

Give the children their bags and show them how to stuff their bags with wadded up newspaper. When each bag is nearly full, fold over the top and staple it closed. This makes the clown's body.

Then let the children use the shapes to trace the clown's head, eyes, nose, mouth, and hat on different colors of construction paper. When they have cut these out, they should glue them together. One cotton ball should be glued at the top of the hat.

Help children attach their assembled clown "heads" to their bag bodies with a stapler. Be sure that the words, "Get Along Together," face the front.

LOVE MAGNETS

10

$\mathbf{A}$head of time cut out two hearts for each child. Make them about 5" in diameter.

Distribute the hearts and magnetic strips to the children. Have the children glue a magnetic strip across the *back* of each of their hearts.

While the glue is drying, go around to each child and make a 2" circle on a half sheet of white construction paper for each one. Then have the children draw and color pictures of themselves within the circles and cut the circles out. (Some children may have trouble drawing a self-portrait that small. Encourage them in whatever they do. Then have them cut out the circles.)

Next the children should glue their self-portraits to the top left-hand corner of the front side of one heart and put the sticker in the same place on the other heart.

While the children are doing this, circulate among them again printing the words, "Loves You!" on each heart.

This will provide the children with one love magnet to remind them of Jesus' love for them and another love magnet to give away expressing their love for the other person.

THINGS YOU'LL NEED:

- ❏ Two 3" magnetic strips for each child
- ❏ Two hearts for each child cut from brightly colored tag board
- ❏ A sticker of Jesus for each child
- ❏ Glue
- ❏ Markers
- ❏ Crayons
- ❏ White construction paper
- ❏ Scissors

page 15 only

11 LOVE MESSAGE

THINGS YOU'LL NEED:

- ❏ A photocopy of the accompanying page for each child
- ❏ Brightly colored sheets of construction paper
- ❏ Glue
- ❏ Markers
- ❏ Crayons
- ❏ Scissors for each child
- ❏ Yarn
- ❏ Tape

Ahead of time make a photocopy of the accompanying page for each child. Cut off the word strip on each page.

Distribute these materials to the children and instruct them to cut out the word shapes. Then help them match and glue the word shapes over the blank shapes on the "Love Message" sheet—like fitting pieces of a puzzle into shape—to complete the message: "As I love you, love one another."

After that the children can color the message.

You might also have the children glue the love message to a sheet of construction paper and tape a length of yarn to the back so that the message can be hung up.

Love Message

John 13:34

- **CUT HERE** -

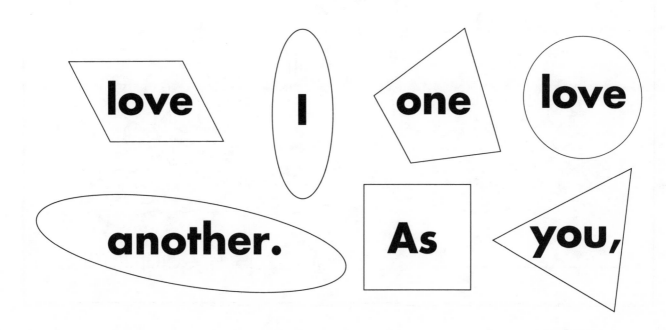

love   I   one   love

another.   As   you,

12 A SPECIAL LAMB

Photocopy the lamb at the bottom of this page onto the bottoms of paper as heavy as your photocopier will accept (probably 30-pound paper). To do this, you will have to cover the top portion of this page with plain paper so these instructions will not be copied, too.

Distribute the lamb pictures to the children and help them press their thumbs into stamp pads, then press their thumbprints in the oval of the lamb's heads. Provide warm soapy water and towels for ink cleanup. Help children print their names to complete the message "_____ is one of God's special lambs."

Explain that God cares so much for each one of us that He has given us each special fingerprints that are not like anyone else's. We are special. Encourage the children to compare their fingerprints, and help by pointing out differences.

Then let the children spread glue on the lambs' bodies and cover them with white polyester quilt batting or cotton balls. Set the completed lambs aside to dry.

Later when lambs have dried, show the children how to fold the paper on the dotted line so that they stand up.

THINGS YOU'LL NEED:

- ❑ A photocopy of the special lamb for each child
- ❑ Inked stamp pads
- ❑ Soapy water and towels
- ❑ Glue
- ❑ Polyester quilt batting or cotton balls

_____ is one of God's special lambs.

I CAN CARE

13

Distribute a photocopy of a project sheet to each child. Instruct the children to cut off the strip of action pictures across the top of the sheet.

Let the children color the hands and the pictures, and talk about the caring actions shown in the pictures that they might do to express care for others.

While the children are coloring the pictures circulate among them and assist by carfully cutting open the vertical lines in the palms of the hands. (These slits may be difficult to cut neatly without sharp scissors, which could be dangerous for your children to use.)

Help the children weave the picture strips into the "caring hands" slits—from the back side to the front and then out the back again—so that they can slide them back and forth displaying the different pictures.

To prevent the strip from slipping out of the slits too easily, fold over the 1/4" free portion on each end of the strip.

THINGS YOU'LL NEED:

❑ A photocopy of the caring hands and the action pictures for each child
❑ Crayons or markers
❑ Scissors

I Can Care

I Can Care

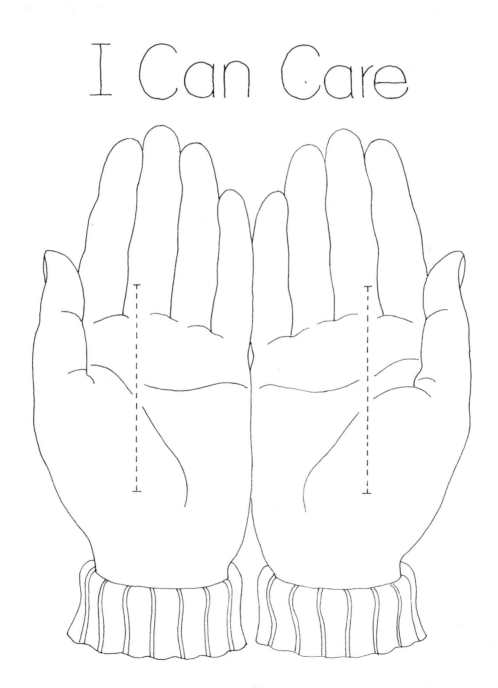

18

CHRISTMAS REMINDER

14

Reproduce the framed message for each child. Let each child cut out a picture reminder from an old Christmas card and glue it over the indicated space on the frame.

Help the children glue a yarn boarder around the Christmas card illustration.

Help children enclose pieces of cardboard in colorful Christmas wrapping paper, and glue the card and message onto this stiff backing.

Punch a hole though the card near the top and tie a loop of yarn through it so that the reminder can be hung if desired.

THINGS YOU'LL NEED:

❑ Old Christmas cards
❑ Wrapping paper
❑ 8 1/2 x 11" pieces of cardboard
❑ Glue
❑ Yarn
❑ Hole punch

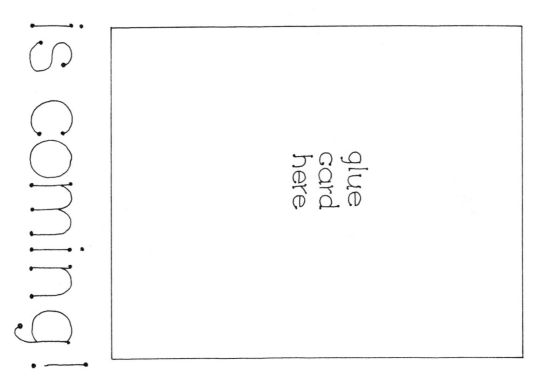

glue
card
here

Christmas is coming!

X

15 GOD MADE FAMILIES PUZZLE

THINGS YOU'LL NEED:

❑ Photocopies of the accompanying puzzle picture
❑ Pieces of light-weight cardboard
❑ Glue or rubber cement
❑ Clear, adhesive-backed shelf paper (optional)
❑ Crayons or markers
❑ Envelopes

Reproduce the illustrated puzzle picture for each child. Before the session, use glue or rubber cement to affix each puzzle sheet to a same-sized piece of light-weight cardboard.

Let children use crayons or markers to color their puzzles.

Optional: Cover each colored puzzle with a piece of clear, adhesive-backed shelf paper. This takes extra time, but it preserves the colors and makes the puzzles more durable.

Cut the puzzles apart along the thin lines designating the puzzle pieces and supervise the children as they put their pieces in envelopes with their names on them. Some children who are very dexterous may be able to cut apart their own puzzles, but the laminated sheets will make the puzzles fairly thick and hard to cut.

God Made Families

THE BEST CHRISTMAS GIFT ORNAMENT

Make a photocopy of baby Jesus for each child. Let children cut out the illustrations and use crayons or markers to color the picture.

Cut out 5" x 6" inch pieces of tag board or heavy construction paper for each child. Help the children glue Christmas gift wrapping paper to cover both sides of the cardboard rectangle.

Have the children glue their pictures of Jesus in the center of the decorated cardboard.

Glue ribbon around the edges of the square to look like a gift. Punch a hole through the top and thread ribbon through the hole and tie a nice bow that will both look like a gift and be useful for hanging the ornament.

THINGS YOU'LL NEED:

- ❏ Photocopies of baby Jesus in the manger
- ❏ Pieces of tagboard
- ❏ Glue or rubber cement
- ❏ Crayons or markers
- ❏ Wide package-wrapping ribbon

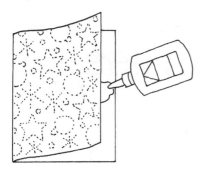  

17 SHEPHERD'S CHRISTMAS GREETING

THINGS YOU'LL NEED:

- ❏ Photocopies of the shepherd picture
- ❏ Glue
- ❏ Cotton balls
- ❏ Yarn or straws
- ❏ Scraps of cloth
- ❏ Crayons or markers

Make copies of the shepherd picture for each child.

Let the children color the background—hills, sky, and town. Encourage them to use a dark crayon or marker to trace the letters of the message in the speech balloon.

Help the children add material to the picture to give it texture and a three-dimensional effect. Glue cotton balls onto the sheep for wool, scraps of material onto the shepherd for clothes, and a straw or brown yarn over the shepherd's staff. (Tip: Glue won't end up where it shouldn't be so easily if it is applied to the picture rather than the materials.)

WISE MEN'S CROWNS AND CHRISTMAS STAR

18

Help children make special Christmas reminders.

• *Crowns*—Create cardboard shapes for a crown according to the accompanying illustration. Design the cardboard shapes so half the zig-zag for the crown will extend above and half below the center line of a sheet of construction paper (lengthwise). This will allow each sheet to make two strips for a crown, which when stapled together will fit around a child's head.

Once the children have selected what color of construction paper they want for their crowns, help them use a cardboard shape to trace the zig-zag edge down the middle. After the children cut apart their crown strips, tape or staple one set of ends together. Then help them fold up the bottom 1" edge (for strength).

Measure the strip around each child's head and cut off the excess allowing a 1" overlap.

Let the children decorate their crowns by gluing on tiny buttons, glitter, pieces of foil or cellophane, sequins, and yarn.

When the glue has dried, staple the remaining ends together to complete the crown.

• *Stars*—Reproduce the star pattern on sheets of construction paper or paper as heavy as your photocopier will accept with manual feed. Let the children cut out their stars. Help children make a boarder of glue around the edge of their stars and lightly sprinkle glitter over the glue. (Place newspaper under the stars to catch excess glitter.)

When the glue is dry, staple or glue the star to a craft stick.

THINGS YOU'LL NEED:

- ❑ Cardboard shape for a crown
- ❑ Various colors of construction paper
- ❑ Scissors
- ❑ Stapler or clear plastic tape
- ❑ Glue
- ❑ Tiny buttons
- ❑ Glitter
- ❑ Aluminum foil or cellophane
- ❑ Sequins
- ❑ Yarn
- ❑ Craft sticks

19 A PRAISE CRAYON HOLDER

THINGS YOU'LL NEED:

- ❏ One and a half paper plates for each child
- ❏ Pencils
- ❏ Crayons or colored markers
- ❏ Glue
- ❏ Cotton balls
- ❏ Scissors
- ❏ Stapler
- ❏ Hole punch
- ❏ Brightly colored yarn or ribbon

In advance, cut half of the paper plates in half.

Distribute one and a half paper plates to each child. Have them draw a line across the middle of the whole plate and then color hills, sky, and sun on the upper half and water with fish in it on the lower half. Help the children paste or glue cotton balls onto the sky to make fluffy clouds. (This may be accomplished most neatly by putting puddles of glue in jar lids. The children can then dip one side of a cotton into the glue and then attach it to their plates.)

Show the children how to cut "waves" along the cut edge of their half plates. Then help them by printing the words, "Praise God for His Power and Care," below the waves.

Let the children staple the half plates to the whole plates making pockets of the space between. They should then punch a hole in the top center of their crayon holders and thread a piece of yarn or ribbon through the hole so they can be hung on a door or some other convenient place at home.

HAPPY HANDS
PRAISE RATTLES

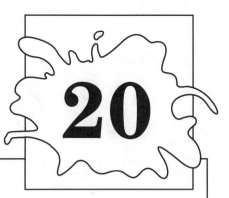

Allow each child to make ink prints of their hands on the bottoms of two plates. Then help the children clean their hands with soap and water while they give the ink a few moments to set.

Tell them that their handprints are something special that God gave them and that no one else in the world has a handprint exactly like theirs.

Show the children how to place a *very thin* line of glue around the rim of both plates. Then distribute about a dozen dried beans to each child and tell them to put the beans in the center of one plate, being careful not to get any glue on the beans.

Have the children turn the other plate upside down and position it directly on the one with the beans, rim-to-rim, creating a cavity between the two plates for the beans, with the handprints on the outside.

After the glue has set a minute or two, staple the rims together for a more secure seal. Using a marker, put each child's name on his or her rattle under a handprint.

Encourage the children shake the rattles in time to music as they praise the Lord.

THINGS YOU'LL NEED:

❑ Two paper plates for each child
❑ About a dozen dried beans for each child
❑ Two or three inked stamp pads
❑ Soapy water and towels for clean up
❑ Glue
❑ Stapler
❑ Black marker

21 PRAISE GOD PARTY HATS

THINGS YOU'LL NEED:

❑ A brightly colored sheet of construction paper for each child
❑ Black marker
❑ Strips of colored tissue paper
❑ Tape
❑ Stapler
❑ Stickers
❑ Glue
❑ Glitter
❑ Two 10" strips of ribbon or yarn for each child

1. Make a broad cone from a sheet of colored construction paper.

2. Tape the cone closed with a *small* piece of tape (A).

3. Cut off the bottom edge of the cone to make it even.

4. Draw a line up the cone with a marker along the joint so that the edge of the paper *and* the backing paper are both marked.

5. Remove the tape and allow the paper to unroll into a flat sheet.

6. Have children decorate their hats with stickers and glitter. Avoid decorating the small backing section (B).

7. Write the words, "God Loves Me," around the base of the hat.

8. Reroll the cones so that the marker lines match and then retape it securely with a longer piece of tape.

9. Make tassels for tops of hats by cutting slits in strips of tissue paper (C).

10. Roll the paper to form tassels and tape to the tops of the hats.

11. Staple ribbon or yarn onto each side of the hats to form ties (D).

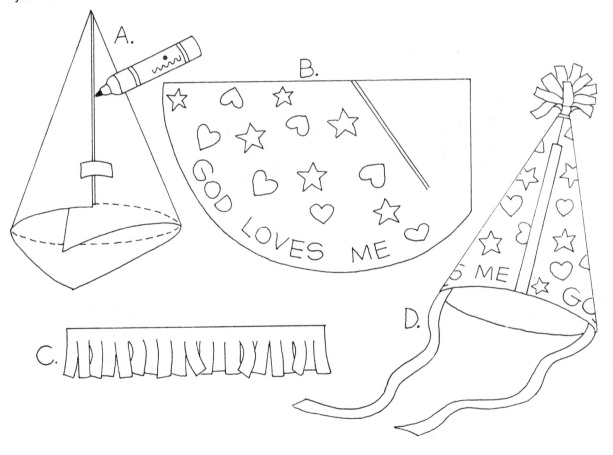

PRAISE PUPPETS

Reproduce the puppet face pattern for each child on white paper. Have the children color the face for the puppet.

Then have them cut it out and cut it in two along the dotted line (the mouth line).

Direct the children to glue the top of the puppet's head to the bottom of the paper lunch bag and the bottom of the face to the side of the bag where it will meet evenly when the bag is folded as shown in the illustration. This will allow the puppet to "talk" when finished.

Allow a few minutes for the glue to dry before use.

Suggest that the children use their puppets to represent the lame man that Jesus healed beside the pool at Bethesda as reported in John 5:1-15. They can make their puppet praise God like the lame man did after Jesus healed him.

THINGS YOU'LL NEED:

❑ Photocopies of the accompanying puppet face
❑ A paper lunch bag for each child
❑ Crayons or markers
❑ Scissors
❑ Glue

23 GIVING MONEY BAGS!

THINGS YOU'LL NEED:

- ❑ A felt circle, about 12" in diameter, for each child
- ❑ A paper or leather hole punch
- ❑ A 15" piece of yarn or a shoelace with plastic tips for each child
- ❑ Several large, plastic, yarn needles (unless shoelaces are used)
- ❑ Black marker with medium tip

Ahead of time, cut out a large felt circle for each child (about 12" in diameter). Punch holes around the edge of the circle—about 1/2" from the edge and 1" apart. (See figure A.)

Use a black marker to print each child's name on what will become the inside bottom of his or her money bag.

Have each child lace yarn through the holes using a plastic needle or use shoelaces with a plastic tip. Help children to tie a knot in each end of their "draw strings" and gently draw the edge together to create a bag. (Figure B.)

Finally tie the strings in a bow to create a finished bag and encourage the children to use the money bag to save their offerings in. (Figure C.)

28

PRAISE GOD BOOKLET

Ahead of time, create a basic booklet for each child. Fold two sheets of 9" X 12" paper in half. Nest one inside the other, and staple them together at the spine to make a four-page booklet (not counting the backs of the pages).

With brightly colored markers, print the following on the cover: "Praise God for Bible Stories." Leave enough room for a child figure in the center of the page. (See illustration.) On the remaining pages, print the following:

(2) At Home

(3) At Church

(4) At Bedtime

Leave enough space on each page for a picture to be drawn.

Prepare a sample booklet with a child figure on page one, a picture of a home on page two, a picture of your church on page three, and moon and stars on page four.

Distribute a booklet to each child. Display your sample and instruct the children to draw and color similar pictures in their booklets. Explain that there are many places where they can praise God by hearing Bible stories.

While the children are drawing and coloring, circulate among them. Compliment them on their work, and help them print their names on the backs of their booklets.

THINGS YOU'LL NEED:

- ❑ Two sheets of 9" X 12" paper for each child
- ❑ Brightly colored markers
- ❑ Crayons
- ❑ Stapler

25 PRAYER COLLAGE

THINGS YOU'LL NEED:

- ❑ Pages torn from magazines of people's faces
- ❑ Yarn or ribbon
- ❑ Hole punch

Ahead of time, draw a figure of a praying child on a 8 1/2" X 11" sheet of paper similar to the above design. Then make a photocopy for each child. Collect numerous pages torn from magazines of people's faces. Include all ages and races.

Distribute a photocopy of the praying child to each child. Have the children turn the figure face down on the table in front of them.

Then have the children cut out faces of people from magazines and glue them onto the back of the praying child figure. The faces can/should overlap so that they look like a crowd of people.

When the glue has dried sufficiently, have the children turn their papers over and cut out the praying child shape.

Punch a small hole in the top of the head. Thread yarn or ribbon through the hole. Tie it so that the collage can be hung to remind them to pray for other people. Help the children print their name's on the backs of their collages.

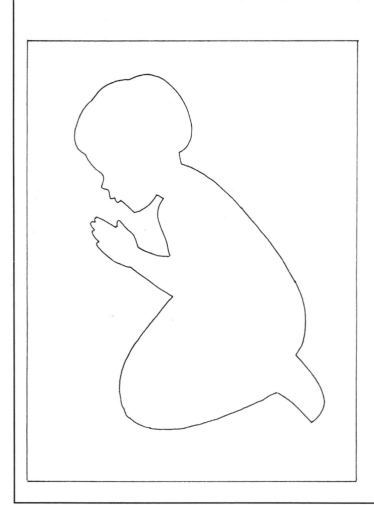

PRAISE INSTRUMENTS PICTURE!

26

Photocopy a set of musical instrument pictures for each child from the accompany patterns.

Give each child a set of instrument pictures and a sheet of colored construction paper.

Show the children how to *tear* out their instrument shapes to create torn pictures. Some children might be uncomfortable tearing out the shapes, thinking that they should cut them with scissors to make clean lines. But you can help them enjoy the process of making shapes this way.

When they have torn out the instrument shapes, have them glue them to their sheet of construction paper and color the instruments.

While the children are coloring their instruments, circulate among them, encouraging them on their work. Also, across the top of each child's sheet print with a bright marker: "Timmy (each child's name) Can Praise God." And across the bottom print: "Through Music!"

THINGS YOU'LL NEED:

- ❑ Copies of the musical instrument patterns
- ❑ Sheets of colored construction paper
- ❑ Brightly colored markers
- ❑ Glue

A ZACCHAEUS TREE

Distribute sheets of light blue and brown construction paper to each child. Instruct the children to use the cardboard shapes to trace tree trunks onto the brown construction paper.

Once they have cut out their "trees," have the children glue them onto the light blue sheets of construction paper.

Have ready green tempera paint in small, flat containers such as jar lids. Cut the sponges into small leaf shapes or rectangles and show the children how to clip one with a clothespin so that the clothespin functions as a handle. Then dip the sponge into the paint and dab it onto the tree limbs to create leaves.

While the children are finishing their project, circulate among them and print across the top with a black marker the title: "Zacchaeus Tree."

Tell the children that they can use their Zacchaeus trees to help them remember the story of Zacchaeus.

Use the soapy water and paper towels to clean up.

crumple tissue paper on end of pencil & stick on tops of tree

THINGS YOU'LL NEED:

- ❑ Sheets of light blue and brown construction paper
- ❑ Cardboard shapes of tree trunks with limbs
- ❑ Pencils
- ❑ Scissors
- ❑ Glue
- ❑ Sponges
- ❑ Clip-type clothespins
- ❑ Green tempera paint
- ❑ Jar lids
- ❑ Large, black marker
- ❑ Soapy water and paper towels

28 NEW LIFE

THINGS YOU'LL NEED:

- ❑ Light colored construction paper
- ❑ Photocopies of "rocks" from accompanying patterns
- ❑ Staples and stapler
- ❑ 5" x 5" piece of aluminum window screen
- ❑ Old toothbrushes
- ❑ Gray or brown tempera paint
- ❑ Paint smocks
- ❑ Small stickers of plants, flowers, baby animals, etc.
- ❑ Plenty of old newspaper
- ❑ Soapy water and paper towels

just color

Give each child a photocopy of a rock and a sheet of light colored construction paper. Have the children cut out the rock and center the rock on the sheet of construction paper. Then help them staple the *top* (only) of the rock to the paper.

Clothe the children with paint smocks. Team each one up with a partner. Give each pair a 5" x 5" piece of window screen and a toothbrush.

Have the children work over tables and floor areas that have been protected from paint by old newspapers. Tell them to take turns spatter painting their paper. One child will hold the screen over the paper with the "rock" stapled to it. The other child will dip the toothbrush in gray or brown tempera paint and brush it over the screen surface, causing spatters of paint to nearly cover the rock and the surrounding paper.

Then have the children leave the project while their papers dry. While they are occupied elsewhere, place a "new life" sticker (flowers, baby animals, etc.) under each rock.

When the children are ready to go home, have them look under the rock to discover the "new life" pictured there.

Remind them of the amazing things God can do and how He provides new life. If it is not possible to surprise the children, distribute stickers and allow them to apply their own. They can then show them to other children as a surprise.

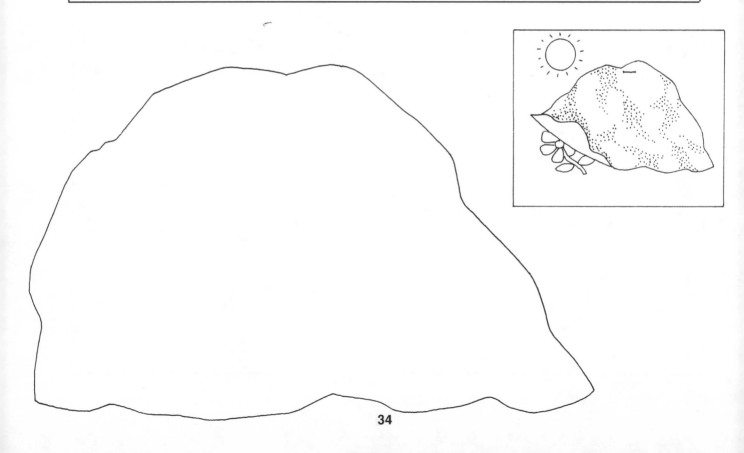

JESUS IS KING!

Ahead of time, cut a slit lengthwise down the middle of one side of each shoe box.

Distribute photocopies of the donkey and Jesus figures and have the children color and cut them out. Help the children glue their figures onto the top portion of craft sticks. Set figures and sticks aside to dry.

Give each child a prepared shoe box. The slit side will become the bottom of the shoe box diorama—the "road" down which the donkey and Jesus can travel. The figure will slide through this slit to move back and forth. Tell the children to set the box on the table with the slit side down.

Depending on the time available and the children's skill, the inside of the box may be decorated. It can simply be painted: blue sky on the top and upper back, brown hills on the lower back, and green grass on the bottom. For added realism, make a winding path of glue on the bottom and cover it with sand. Cut out palm trees from green construction paper and buildings from brown construction paper to be glued onto the background of the shoe box diorama.

Help the children insert the sticks of their figures through the slits. Show them how to use the stick to move the donkey along the road.

THINGS YOU'LL NEED:

- ❏ Photocopies of the donkey and Jesus figure on paper as heavy as your copier will accept
- ❏ A shoe box for each child
- ❏ Sand

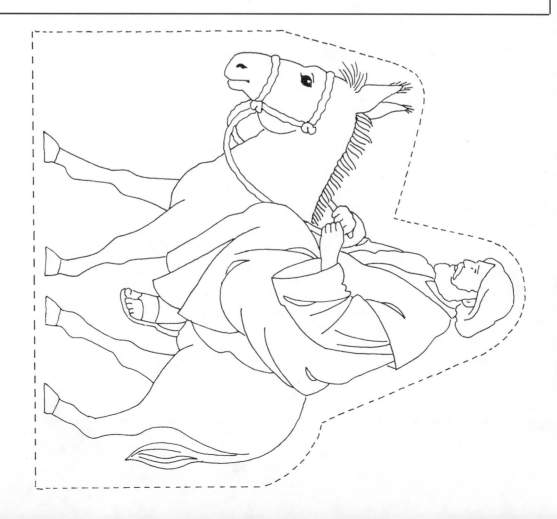

30 BUTTERFLY

THINGS YOU'LL NEED:

❏ Nonclip clothespins
❏ 5" x 8" sheets of pastel tissue paper
❏ Black chenille wire

Give each child a wooden, nonclip clothespin, two different colors of 5" x 8" pieces of pastel tissue paper, and a black chenille wire.

Show the children how to wrap the chenille wire around the top nob of the clothespin to make antennae. Help the children make the butterfly wings by pushing two different colored sheets of tissue paper into the split in the clothespin until it is gathered near the top.

PRAISE WINDSOCK

Distribute a strip of light-weight cardboard, cut from manila file folders, about 3" x 11", to each child. Tell the children to draw a cross, a rock, a cloud, and a crown on their strips. (You might draw simple examples on the chalk-board or flip chart.)

While the children are drawing the figures on the strips, arrange piles of crepe paper streamers by color so that the children can pick up one streamer of each color.

Then have the children collect sets of streamers and staple an end of each one to the *under side* of their cardboard strips. The streamers should be spaced so that a rainbow effect is achieved across the whole length of the strip.

Then show the children how to roll the strip—streamers inside and drawings outside—into a cylinder, overlapping and stapling the ends together.

Distribute three lengths of yarn to each child. Instruct children to tie a small knot at the end of each piece of yarn. (Do not tie the lengths together yet.) Then they should staple the knotted end of each length of yarn to the inside of the cylinder, extending out the opposite way from the streamers. The yarn lengths should be positioned equidistant from each other around the cylinder.

Help the children draw all three pieces of yarn out, tying them together with one knot in their free ends. This will also provide a point from which the windsock can be hung.

THINGS YOU'LL NEED:

- ❑ Crepe paper streamers in the colors of the rainbow, about two feet long
- ❑ Strips of light-weight cardboard, cut from manila file folders, about 3" X 11"
- ❑ Several staplers
- ❑ Colorful yarn in 15" lengths
- ❑ Crayons or markers

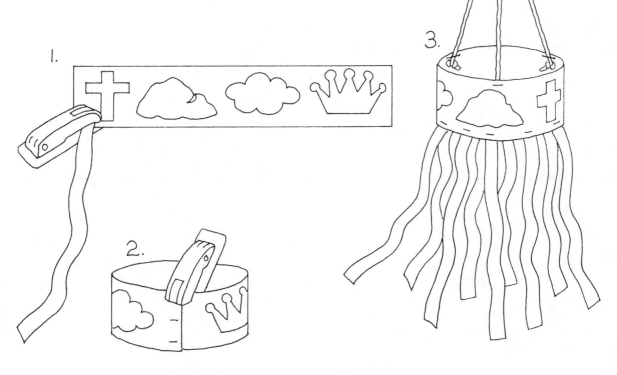

32 SHARING-CAN-BE-FUN KIDS

THINGS YOU'LL NEED:

- ❑ Photocopies of the sharing kids patterns
- ❑ Scissors
- ❑ Crayons
- ❑ Brass paper fasteners
- ❑ Hole punch

Photocopy the design below of the boy, girl, and "arm." Use paper as heavy as your photocopier will accept.

Distribute one copy and one brass paper fastener to each child. Have the children color the pictures and then cut off the right strip containing the arm. They should then cut out the arm.

Circulate among the children punching a hole in the arm at the X. Then show the children how to put the paper fastener through the hole and into the larger pictures at the point of the X to attach the arm to the girl's body. Fold over the fasteners, and help the children to carefully move the arm the first time or two so that it does not tear out.

Tell the children that the girl is sharing a cookie with her friend. She has made him happy. Remind them that sharing is one way to show Jesus' love. Sharing makes us happy, too. Sharing with others makes Jesus happy.

SHARING CAN BE FUN

38

SHARING CAN BE FUN

33 PLACE MAT

THINGS YOU'LL NEED:

- ❑ Photocopies of the place mat designs
- ❑ Scissors
- ❑ Crayons
- ❑ Happy-face and flower stickers
- ❑ Clear, plastic, adhesive shelf paper, 10" wide

Using 8 1/2" x 14" paper, create a photocopyable place mat master similar to the illustration. With a marker, print the words: "Jesus Loves You" across the top, and across the bottom: "And I Do, Too!" followed by a line. The blank line after the bottom words is for the children to enter their own name. Draw a heart, a few simple flowers, or any other design on the master. Photocopy enough of these so that each child can have one.

Distribute the photocopies to the children and have them color the mats, enter their names on the line (assisting as necessary), and decorate them with stickers.

Then cover the mat, front and back, with clear, plastic, adhesive shelf paper at least 10" wide. Allow it to extend 1" on each end so that the mat is laminated between the plastic protection.

Have the children trim off the excess plastic leaving about 1/2" on all sides.

CLEAR ADHESIVE SHELF PAPER

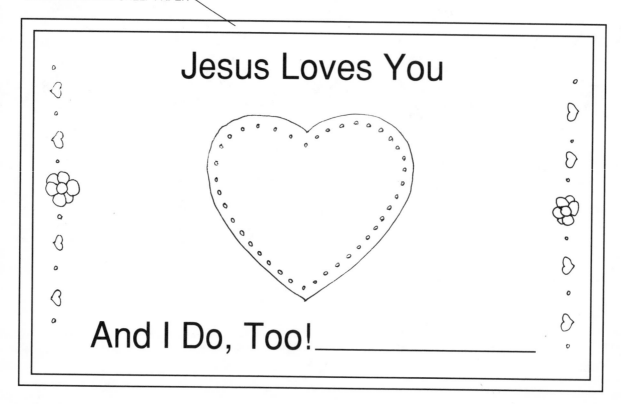

40

GIVEAWAY BOOKMARK

In advance, prepare several heart-shaped cardboard patterns about 2" wide. Have the children use pencils to trace around the cardboard heart patterns onto brightly colored construction paper. Then each child should cut out a heart. Help the children print on their hearts the words: "Jesus Loves You!" On the back they can print: "From (and then their name)."

Then assist the children in cutting a length of ribbon for themselves about 5" long. It will look best if one end is cut square and the other end on a 45-degree angle.

Help the children staple their hearts to their ribbons as shown in the illustration.

Tell the children that their bookmarks can be gifts. They could be given to someone who does not know about Jesus, or they could be given as reminders to anyone that Jesus loves them. Encouraging the children to give away the bookmark, reinforces the idea that young children can help others know about Jesus.

THINGS YOU'LL NEED:

❑ Cardboard heart patterns
❑ Pencils
❑ Brightly colored, ribbon (1" or wider)
❑ Stapler
❑ Markers
❑ Scissors
❑ Brightly colored construction paper

JESUS LOVES YOU

35 ASK-ME-ABOUT-JESUS BUTTONS

THINGS YOU'LL NEED:

- ❑ Cardboard circles, 3" in diameter
- ❑ Photocopies of the button design
- ❑ Safety pins
- ❑ Tape
- ❑ Stapler
- ❑ Scissors
- ❑ Crayons
- ❑ Glue
- ❑ Stickers of Jesus

In advance, make a photocopy of the button design, and cut out a cardboard 3" circle for each child. Tape a small safety pin to the center of each cardboard circle. Make sure the "pin" side of the safety pin is away from the cardboard and free. Then reinforce the tape by putting a staple through the tape on either side of the safety pin.

Let the children color the words in the designs, cut them out, and glue them to the cardboard backing.

Provide a sticker of Jesus for each child to affix to the button.

Help the children pin their buttons to their dresses or shirts.

Just Color & Decorate

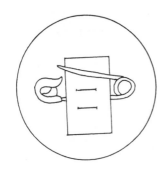

PAUL AND BARNABAS

Distribute two craft sticks and a Paul and a Barnabas figure to each child. Direct the children to color their men.

Have the children put their names on each craft stick. Or do this for them while they are coloring their figures.

Then show the children how to glue or tape their figures onto craft sticks.

THINGS YOU'LL NEED:

- ❑ Photocopies of Paul and Barnabas on paper as heavy as your copier will accept
- ❑ Craft sticks
- ❑ Glue or tape
- ❑ Crayons or markers

PAUL

BARNABAS

43

37 THANK YOU BANNER

THINGS YOU'LL NEED:

- ❏ Photocopies of the pictures of a pastor, teacher, and parents
- ❏ Photocopies of the "message" phrases
- ❏ Brightly colored ribbon or strips of construction paper, 2" x 11"
- ❏ Stapler
- ❏ Glue
- ❏ Crayons and/or markers
- ❏ 10" lengths of yarn

Distribute photocopies of the pictures of a pastor, teacher, and parents to each child. While children are coloring and cutting out the pictures, distribute a strip of ribbon or construction paper to each child.

Help the children by folding over the top inch of the ribbon and stapling it to create a small loop through which the yarn hanger will pass.

When the children are finished coloring the pictures, distribute the message phrases. Then show them how to glue the "Thank You, God, for . . ." phrase to the top of the banners followed by the three pictures and the concluding phrase, "Who teach us about You," at the bottom.

Have the children thread the yarn through the loops and tie them.

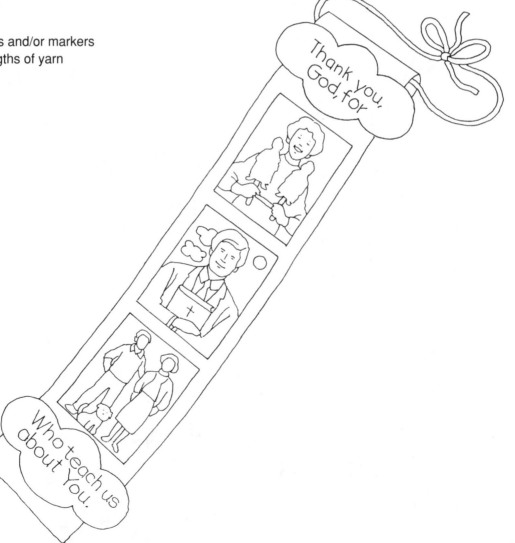

Thank you,
God, for

Who teach us
about You.

38 THINKING-OF-YOU CARD

THINGS YOU'LL NEED:

❑ Photocopies of the card designs
❑ Crayons and/or markers
❑ Scissors
❑ Sheets of colored construction paper cut 8" x 8"
❑ #10 size business envelopes

Distribute copies of card design to each child. The children should color the messages and cut them out.

Have the children glue the messages onto pieces of folded construction paper as per example. Help them make sure the outside message is on the outside and right side up and the inside message is put inside, right side up.

Guide the children in signing their names at the end of the greetings.

The children should put their cards in envelopes and get them ready to deliver or mail.

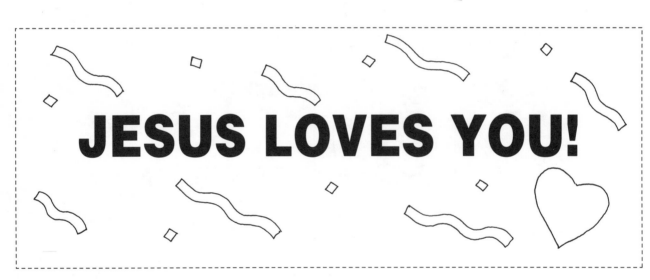

pg 48

JESUS LOVES YOU

Make a photocopy of the booklet pages sheet for each child. Help the children fold their sheets along the dotted lines so that the words, "Know What?" appear on the cover; the picture of Jesus is on page 2; the dotted-lined words, "Loves You," are on page 3; and the words, "That's Good News!" appear on the back.

Have the children color the picture of Jesus, trace over the dotted-lined words on page three, and color in the words on the back.

Happy-face stickers can decorate the front or back.

THINGS YOU'LL NEED:

❑ Photocopies of the booklet pages sheet
❑ Crayons or markers
❑ Happy-face stickers

PAGE 3   PAGE 2

LOVES YOU

THAT'S GOOD NEWS!

KNOW WHAT?

BACK   COVER

KNOW WHAT?

47

KNOW
WHAT?

THAT'S
GOOD
NEWS!

LOVES
YOU

PAPER LUNCH BOX

40

Fold a page from a wallpaper sample book in half (or substitute a large sheet of construction paper). Trace the pattern of the lunch box on the paper with the side marked "fold" on the fold of the paper. Cut out the lunch box through both thicknesses; use fingernail or other small scissors for cutting out the opening in the handle. Print, "Thank You, God, for My Lunch," on the outside. Pass out magazine pictures of various foods and beverages and let children choose some of their favorites. Help children cut these out and glue them inside their lunch boxes.

THINGS YOU'LL NEED:

- ❑ Copy of lunch box pattern
- ❑ Wallpaper sample pages or construction paper
- ❑ Magazine pictures of various foods
- ❑ Scissors
- ❑ Paste

FOLD

49

41

STRAW PRAYER REMINDER

THINGS YOU'LL NEED:

❑ Copies of raindrop pattern, *or* a cardboard raindrop shape for children to trace
❑ Light blue construction paper (if needed)
❑ Hole punch
❑ Plastic straws
❑ Plastic wrap

Give each child a copy of the raindrop pattern to color and cut out. Or show children how to trace a cardboard pattern of the raindrop on light blue construction paper and cut it out. Help the children punch two holes as indicated on the raindrop pattern, so they can insert a drinking straw. If the raindrop is traced onto construction paper, print "Thank You, God, for Water" on the raindrop with permanent marker. Now help children thread the raindrop onto a straw, leaving just enough straw at the top so that it can be used to drink without putting the paper raindrop in the mouth. The straw prayer reminder can be wrapped in plastic wrap so it will stay clean on the way home.

When children use this straw to have a drink, they can remember to thank God for giving us water!

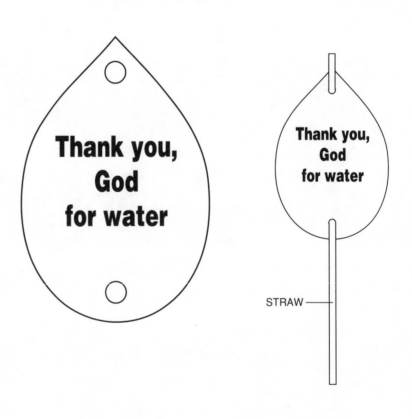

'GOD IS WITH ME' BACKPACK

42

Children can make simple backpacks to carry their things.

Give each child a paper grocery bag. (Bags a little smaller than the size commonly used for packing groceries are best, but larger ones work also.) Fold *to the inside* a 2" edge around the top of the bag. Cut a piece of yarn about a yard long and tie the ends tightly together. Grasp the resulting loop of yarn in the center, forming a sideways figure-eight. Staple the yarn securely at that center point to the folded top edge of the bag on one side, forming two loops that a child can put his or her arms through when putting on the backpack.

On the other side of the bag print the words, "God Goes with Me Wherever I Go." Children can decorate the bags with crayon designs or pictures of places they would like to go. Tell children they can use their backpacks to carry things that aren't too heavy.

THINGS YOU'LL NEED:

❑ Paper bags from the grocery store
❑ Heavy yarn (one yard per child)
❑ Stapler
❑ Markers, crayons

God Goes With Me Wherever I Go

43 SUN VISOR

THINGS YOU'LL NEED:

- ❑ Large paper plates
- ❑ White elastic (1/4" wide)
- ❑ Scissors
- ❑ Markers and crayons
- ❑ Stapler
- ❑ Tissue paper (optional)

Cut visors from large white paper plates, using the pattern on this page or following the diagram. Write "God Does What He Promises" across the top of each one. Encourage the children to decorate their visors, asking them to avoid covering up the writing. If the paper plates have a fluted edge, the children could color along the fluting lines (try red and blue on the white plates for an Independence Day visor). Or they could "squash" one-inch squares of red and blue tissue around an index finger and then glue them onto the visors.

When the decorating is finished, cut a piece of 1/4" white elastic to go across the back of each child's head, making the elastic short enough that it will hold the visor firmly in place. Staple the elastic securely to the two corners of the plate.

A GIVING WELL

44

This craft will help children tell the story of Isaac, who trusted God to give him water when others took away his wells. *Background:* Genesis 26:12-25.

For each child prepare a 7 oz. translucent plastic cup with a 1" hole cut out of the bottom, a 3"-4" doughnut shape cut from brown construction paper with a 1" hole cut out of the center, a 4" square cut from a white plastic garbage bag, a rubber band, and a copy of the four story pieces.

Work with the cup upside down. Show children how to coat the surface around the 1" hole on the bottom of the cup with white glue. Center the brown doughnut-shaped well rim so the hole in it lines up with the hole in the bottom of the cup; press together and turn the cup right side up.

Cover the large opening of the cup with the square of white plastic. Hold it in place with the rubber band. Help the children stretch the plastic tight like a drum.

Turn the cup upside down again; this is the "giving" well. Now let the children cut out the four story pieces. Explain that these will go in the well as the story is told of Isaac and his wells as follows:

Mound of dirt—This is the dirt people put in Isaac's wells, to make him move away.

Shovel—Isaac's servants kept digging new wells wherever Isaac went with his family.

Water drop—God provided water in the wells wherever Isaac went. God provided water for everyone—even Isaac's enemies.

Heart—Isaac showed love and kindness toward the people who took away his wells. He believed God would take care of him.

THINGS YOU'LL NEED:

- ❑ Copies of the story pieces
- ❑ Translucent plastic cups (7 oz. size)
- ❑ Brown construction paper
- ❑ White plastic garbage bags
- ❑ Rubber bands
- ❑ White glue

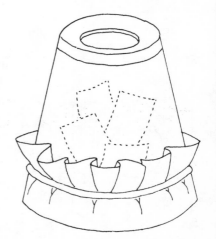

45 CHANGING FACES

THINGS YOU'LL NEED:

- ❏ Three copies of the face for each child
- ❏ Scissors
- ❏ Crayons or markers
- ❏ Tape or paste
- ❏ ~~Large blank circle stickers or labels~~

In advance, photocopy page 55. Make three copies of the face page for each child.

Children can color the eyes and hair on their faces (should be the same for all three). Girls might want to add more length to the hair. Then show children how to add a sad mouth to one face, a sad mouth and tears to another face, and a happy, smiling mouth to the third face. Help children fold all the faces in half vertically. Tape or paste the face with tears to half of the sad face page and the other half to the smiling face page (back to back). Then tape the other half of the sad face page and the smiling face page together (back to back). See diagram.

Give each child three ~~blank circle stickers or labels~~. Help them print the following words on the stickers: I AM SORRY, I AM FORGIVEN, I AM HAPPY AGAIN. Put the stickers on the appropriate face pages.

Make up some "What If . . ." situations about being forgiven or forgiving someone. Tell children to hold up their faces and change them to show appropriate expressions to go along with the story.

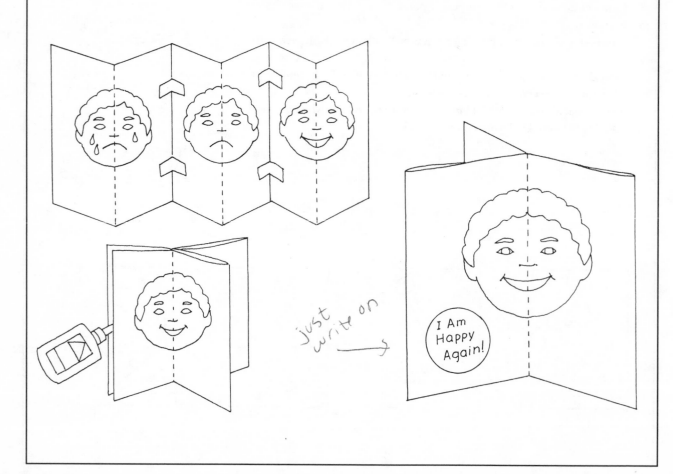

just write on →

I Am Happy Again!

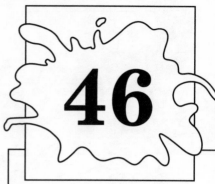

46 ROYAL HANDS

THINGS YOU'LL NEED:

❏ Construction paper in assorted light colors
❏ Crayons or felt-tip markers
❏ Small paper hearts or heart stickers
❏ Paste
❏ Small crown stickers (optional)
❏ Scissors (if needed)

Help children trace one hand with fingers spread apart on a half piece of construction paper with a crayon or felt-tip marker. Give each child five crown stickers to put on the tip of each finger; or help children draw crowns on the tip of each finger. Then show children how to draw a face on each finger beneath the crown. Add a heart sticker or paper heart on the palm of the hand.

As you work, talk about ways we can use our "royal hands" to treat others as a kind king or queen would.

just. make a drawing that resembles

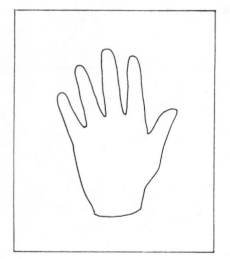

royal hands

BIG IMPRESSIONS

Make photocopies of the shapes shown here and cut out. (Or use shapes as a pattern and trace onto construction paper; cut out.) Give each child a sheet of white paper. Show children how to lay a paper shape on the table (a bit of rolled cellophane tape on the back may hold it in place) and cover it with the white paper. Then rub over the shape under the paper with the side of a crayon. The harder you rub, the brighter the image. Tell the children to hold the paper as still as they can while rubbing.

Once the first impression is made, move the shape to a new spot under the white paper. Use another color and rub again. Try other shapes. Overlap colors. Mount finished "big impressions" on a sheet of construction paper if desired.

As you work, talk about how the shapes may seem like little things but they are important in big ways:

Stars—look small to us but they're really big.

Hearts—a caring heart can give a lot of love.

Birds—they may be small but they are important to God.

Hands—small hands can do great things with God's help.

Diamonds—are small but they're worth a lot of money.

THINGS YOU'LL NEED:

❑ Sheet of white paper for each child
❑ Copies of shapes (star, bird, etc.) to trace
❑ Crayon pieces without paper on them
❑ Scissors
❑ Cellophane tape (optional)
❑ Construction paper (optional)

make shapes out of poster board

48 CARING GLASSES

THINGS YOU'LL NEED:

❑ Chenille wires in two different colors
❑ Plastic rings from soft drink six-pack holders (optional)

Give each child eight chenille wires in two different colors. (Adjust number depending on length of wires.) Show the children how to twist two colors together. Help children make the eyepieces by making two circles or a figure eight, depending on the length of the chenille wires. Twist the ends together to hold in place. Hold the eyepieces up to the child's face and adjust to fit the bridge of the nose.

Twist two more wires together and attach to one side of the eyepiece. Bend the other end to fit behind the ear. Repeat for the other side. Make sure that no sharp ends are sticking out of the joints. Flatten any points that stick out. Put on the glasses and adjust as needed.

Encourage the children to use the glasses to see things that need care. What can you do to help or show kindness?

Alternative: Instead of chenille wire eyepieces, use two plastic rings cut from a soft drink six-pack holder.

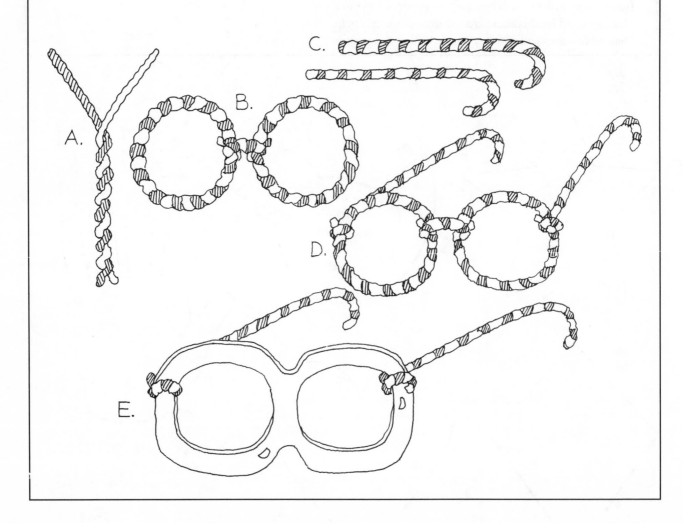

SAD AND HAPPY PUPPETS

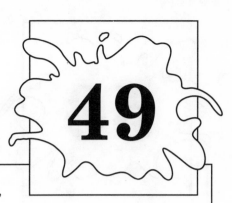

49

With a compass or an object around which you can trace, make two circles, each about 4" in diameter, on an 8 1/2" X 11" sheet of paper. With a black marker, draw a sad and a happy face within them as shown in the accompanying illustration.

Make a photocopy of these faces for each child.

Distribute two paper plates, a craft stick, and a photocopy of the sad and happy faces to each child.

Have the children color and then cut out the sad and happy faces. They should then glue one to the bottom of one plate and the other to the bottom of the second plate. The children can add yarn for hair if they wish.

Show the children how to glue a craft stick to the inside of one of the plates so that 2/3 of it extends beyond the edge of the plate from the "bottom" of that plate's face.

Then help the children staple the two plates together with their faces outward.

The children can flip the puppets back and forth to express how they are feeling, how characters in a story you are telling feel, or how God feels when we do various things.

THINGS YOU'LL NEED:
- ❏ A compass
- ❏ Black marker
- ❏ Photocopies of the sad and happy faces for each child
- ❏ Glue
- ❏ A craft stick for each child
- ❏ Crayons
- ❏ Yarn
- ❏ Two small paper plates for each child
- ❏ Scissors
- ❏ Stapler

50

SURPRISE PICTURES

THINGS YOU'LL NEED:

- ❑ Photocopies of the picture of Jesus for each child
- ❑ Glue
- ❑ Crayons
- ❑ Black marker
- ❑ Construction paper

Photocopy enough pictures of Jesus, so there will be one for each child. Cut on the solid line below.

Prepare a sheet of light-colored construction paper for each child, the same size as the picture of Jesus. Using the dotted line around the Jesus picture as a rough measure, cut a three-sided window in the construction paper. (Don't cut on the dotted line on the Jesus picture.)

Distribute the pictures of Jesus and the pre-cut sheets of construction paper to the children.

Instruct the children to lay the construction paper on top of the picture of Jesus. Then have them glue, tape, or staple the edges together, but make sure there is no glue on the window.

Have the children color the picture of Jesus.

As the children work, circulate among them using a black marker to print: "Who loves _____ ?" above the window, filling in the blank with each child's name.

Let the children open the window to see who loves them.

$ pg 62 only

BRAILLE PLAQUES

Ahead of time photocopy enough of the "Jesus Cares" patterns so that each child can have one. To give the paper enough substance so that the braille dots will stand up, it is important to use 20 pound stationery with a 25 percent cotton content for the photocopied patterns. Carefully fold each sheet in half as indicated and glue it together, applying glue to the *entire* surface.

Distribute one of these Jesus Cares patterns to each child. Have each child draw a picture in the box of a time when he or she needed help.

Then show children how to make the braille dots. Turn the plaque upside down on a soft surface of several layers of felt or a short-nap carpet (or carpet scrap). Using a *dull* pencil, poke holes just barely through the paper at each black dot.

Have the children turn their plaques over and glue them to sheets of colored construction paper cut about one inch larger than the plaque to provide a bright boarder.

Staple a loop of yarn to the top of each plaque for hanging.

Have the children close their eyes and gently glide their fingers across the braille dots without crushing them flat. Explain that this is the way blind people read. See if they can recognize the difference between the letters. It's hard until you learn.

Emphasize for the children that Jesus cares about us when we need help just like He cares for the needs of blind people.

THINGS YOU'LL NEED:

- ❑ Photocopies of the "Jesus Cares" pattern
- ❑ Crayons and/or colored markers
- ❑ Pencils with *dull* points
- ❑ Several layers of felt or short-nap carpet scraps
- ❑ Brightly colored construction paper
- ❑ Glue
- ❑ Colored yarn
- ❑ Stapler

JESUS-IS-NEAR BOOKLETS

52

Reproduce enough "Jesus Is Near" cover sheets for your children. Cut on the solid line and fold on the dotted line. Cut sheets of plain white paper in half, and fold them in half down the center. Insert them in the folded cover sheets; then staple them to make a booklet.

Print "When I travel" on one inside page and "When I sleep" on another.

Have the children complete the pages by drawing themselves sleeping or traveling. On the blank pages, let each child suggest another situation where Jesus is near—in school, day care, or other places where they need to remember Jesus is near. Circulate among the children and print in the names of their personalized situations as they draw pictures of them.

If you prefer, let the children cut out pictures of children's bedrooms and vehicles from old catalogs, and let the children paste these into the booklets.

THINGS YOU'LL NEED:

❑ Photocopies of the "Jesus Is Near" cover sheets for each child
❑ Crayons and/or colored markers
❑ Old magazines and catalogs with pictures of children
❑ Scissors
❑ Stapler

This Book Belongs To...

Jesus Is Near

53 EASTER CROSS BOOKMARKS

Reproduce enough copies of the bookmark design so that each child will have one. Use paper as heavy as your photocopier will accept.

Distribute the designs to the children and have them cut out their crosses.

Let the children color the crosses. They may also add decorations such as glitter, rick-rack, or flower sticker seals.

Help the children print their names on the back of their bookmarks.

To strengthen the bookmarks, you may wish to cover them front and back with clear, adhesive shelf paper. Trim slightly larger than the cross so that the plastic creates a sealed envelope for the cross.

The cross may be used to mark the Easter story in the child's Bible.

THINGS YOU'LL NEED:

❑ Photocopies of the Easter cross bookmark design
❑ Crayons
❑ Easter stickers, glitter, other decorations
❑ Clear, adhesive shelf paper
❑ Scissors

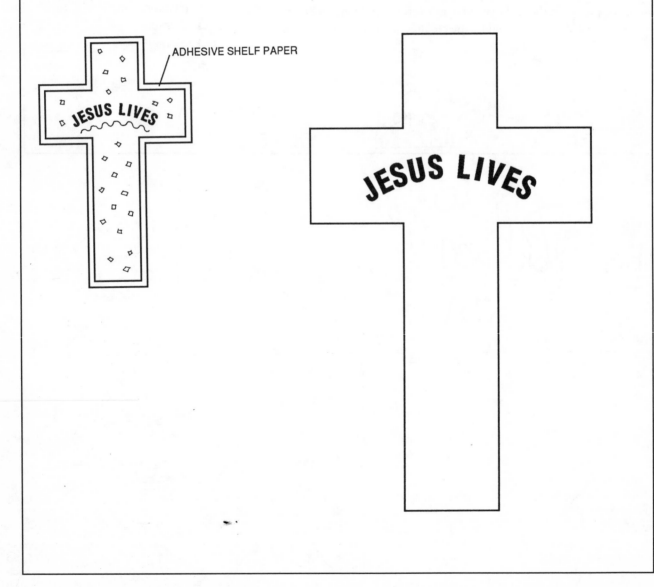

ADHESIVE SHELF PAPER

JESUS LIVES

JESUS LIVES